Assets Of Inspiration

Assets Of Inspiration

Believe Then Achieve

Matthew L. Scigousky

Publisher and wholesale enquiries:
pandelabrapublishing@outlook.com.
www.pandelabrapublishing.com

Pandelabra Publishing
403 West 6th St.
Erie, PA 16507
1.814.806.9172

**Pandelabra
Publishing**

Table of Contents

About The Author

Matthew Lawrence Scigousky was born in the Chicago suburbs and spent his childhood in Lake Tahoe CA. In many ways, he was born into adversity. At six months old he had both legs in casts and was misdiagnosed with MS. As it turns out, a spinal tumor was the real issue. He underwent three spinal surgeries and multiple surgeries on his left leg, all before the age of ten. This left him with a permanently deformed left leg, an adversity that would challenge him his entire life.

There was a choice made at a very young age by Matthew. *"You can do whatever you set your mind to no matter the circumstances."* This became embedded in his soul and has only gotten stronger throughout the years. He became a competitive ski racer in middle school and learned to adapt and compete in other sports such as wrestling in high school and track in college.

After earning his degree in business from DePaul University, Matthew embarked on a career in medical device sales becoming the youngest sales rep ever hired at Stryker Medical and earning 'rookie-of-the year' and 'rep-of-the-year' honors in his first two years. After 25 years in the business and working for other companies such as Merit Medical and Siemens Healthcare he has amassed four 'rep-of-the-year' honors, over a dozen "President Club" awards, and multiple other awards in sales achievement.

Outside of business Matthew enjoys athletics and works out five to six days a week. Most mornings start at 4:30am, pushing his body to do things with one leg that most cannot do with two. Matthew has applied the same principles outlined in this book to training, and maintains a healthy lifestyle balanced with hard work, fun, and enjoying all that life has to offer.

Something challenging happened when Matthew was forty-six years old, the tumor came back after thirty-five years. Matthew underwent a seven-hour spinal surgery and spent five days recovering at the hospital. His positive mindset and belief system within this book propelled him to a recovery his doctor was simply amazed with. He walked out of the hospital on day five completely off pain medication and is stronger today than ever before. He will tell you that he already knew this would be the outcome and embraced the challenging ordeal with excitement!

Inspiring others to find their true potential and become their best selves has become a passion for Matthew. In his own words he has been truly blessed. His disability is really a gift and if you ask him, he would not change anything that happened. He would not be the man he is today without the adversities offered by his left leg.

His true mission in in life is to pass on all that he has been blessed with, to share with others so they may find the same benefits he has found. The real gift in life is in giving and there is no better gift than to lift others up and show them a way to live an abundant life.

Oxygen

Oxygen
Rare air is what you are
Every inhale breathes life into me
Nothing can compare
A single breath is all it takes
To feel love like no compare
Always and forever you are my air...

Renata,

I made a promise to write you a poem every day for ten days,
this was the first, and lead me to discover a gift inside to share.

Thank you with all my love,
Matthew

When two people are connected in the soul
One always knows when the other needs
them. On 07-26-22 Renata knew I
needed her and saved my life in the process.
I will never forget and love you forever.

The Rising

Shattered, broken, a fall from the
Top of the mountain back down to the bottom
All seems lost at this moment
Removal of everything has occurred by a dismantling
Thoughts of nothingness lend to an

Overwhelming feeling of loss
Vent everything out and look deep into the mirror
Eyes look back at you, seeing yourself exposed and raw
Reflect, for you have been left with the most important thing

That which holds the power to create and no one can take away
Our minds and how we choose to think is the gift you are born
with

Unshackle it from negativity and make the choice to begin again
New fields have been cleared from this wildfire
Lines vector these fields awaiting the seeds of a new crop to
grow
On this day I stare in the mirror and choose me
Clearing away all the things that did not serve me well
Kept are only the good, based on experience

You have been given a gift, as hard as it is to see in this moment
One day you will look back and realize
You had to go through all the pain and struggle to reach new
heights
Removing toxicity will hurt because we fight it

Greatness comes after and the tools needed have been crafted from this fire
Rebuild with them and come back stronger than ever
Each day take a step forward toward what you want
Apply power and never use force
Think about exactly where you want to go
Neutral shifts into drive
Empty tank now filled with purity of purpose
Starting over is not easy and most will fight it, but I promise
Starting over after losing it all with positivity, unlocks your greatness

I know it to be true because I've done it myself
I believe you can too! Start believing in you!

Depth

Dig deep
Investigate areas few will go
Seek new ground
Close in on new growth
Open the door marked fear
Vanquish doubt and walk through
Embrace the feeling
Right now you want to go back
I can't believe I'm about to do this
Escape
Shut those thoughts down now

Arriving at new levels
Requires
Embarking into the depths

Molding new strength and sure will power
Attitude of it must be done
Desire to seek out
Emphasis to go there

Activated by the mind
The line is clear to see

Drive below
Engulfed
Punctuate this moment
True strength is discovered
Harvest all you can

Discoveries are made at depth.

Stronger

Produced by the work put in
Utter discomfort at times
Reciprocity for a higher level
Purpose defined with target sighted
Onset the process
Solitude on this journey
Empty the tank, refill, and repeat

Fortitude to press on
Outlast your sense to stop
Resist the urge for relief

There is something to be gained
However a price must be paid
Earn it by enduring

Pour everything you have into it
Absolute commitment
I except nothing less
Never stop until limits are broken through

Purpose for the pain.

Limit Breaker

Conceive with imagination
Out of bounds go
New idea imagined
Corresponding mental chemistry
Inconceivable to others, afterthought
Empower the mental workshop
Vertical, full thrust
Engage persistence

Believe in your mission
Employ the universe
Let it be your guide
Internal strength to excel
Evolved through pain
Vicious failure, adjust try again!
Each step gets you closer

Achievement is a mindset
Can doesn't end with not
Hold to this standard
Into the abyss
Enter and emerge
Victory at hand
Every stage led to this podium stand

Conceive, Believe, and Achieve.

Asset Of Great Value

Disguised as a limitation

Appearance formed from adversity
Seen initially as a limitation
Strength waiting to be tapped into
Everlasting persistence develops
Thorough analysis, then use imagination

Opens the reservoir of possible
Focuses the mind on solutions

Grace replaces anger once accepted
Reason greater than you to discover
Embrace it as a gift
Attaining heights not imagined
Thankful in so many ways, tears trickle down

Value created, unmeasurable
Abundance in life by those you touch
Limit breaker is your nickname
Use it to aim for what you were made for
Each one of you has this inside. Use it, let me show you how....

Asset of Great Value.

Legendary

Hours, days, years go by
Our hopes and dreams
Will either live or die

Will you take a leap for something greater
Irrelevance is a comfort place
Leave it behind to become
Legendary in your space

Your dedication to a craft impacts
One purpose with a goal to strive
Unabridged this path, now drive

Become what was born within
Embrace the gift, otherwise a sin

Remembered you will be
Enriching lives for all to see
Mastered over time
Effortless and ingrained by the mind
Made by a commitment
Backed by principles of belief
Elevating all who surround
Rewarded is the seeker who is found
Events will be recorded as treasure
Discovering the next legacy to measure

How will you be remembered?

Giving Then Getting

Something people want from you
Pertaining to a gift inside
Educate to help better the receiver
Condition oneself to lift others up
Inspired they will leave you
Appreciative and generous
Learn to master this craft
It will serve not only you but all around
Zeal will grow in multiples
Effortless in delivery
Definitive in purpose

Knowledge put into practice
Not only to give the message
Outdone by being the message
Wielded by experience
Leveraged by practice
Empowering those you touch
Deployed to enrich not only you but
Gracious recipients
Entrusted you have become

Specialized knowledge.

The Vortex

Space of focus and inspiration
Perpetuate this state of mind
Articulations of a frequency formulate
Calculations enter flow
Elevation of ideas formulated

Of clear mind, body, and soul
Finds a track to follow effortlessly

Focus the mind deeply on what you want
Offer gratitude
Continuously repeat these thoughts
Universal energy surrounds
Supporting actions of defined purpose

And responding to faith of that purpose
Nerves tingle all over in the vortex
Dwell in this feeling

Inspiration manifests
Nature and creation in harmony
Seen reality emerges from the unseen
Practice to reflection to wisdom
Iridescent possibilities
Reflect from all areas
Actions and awareness become one
The great work is being done
Increased faith, increases the flow
Opposition melts away
Nucleus of intelligence connects all

Space of Focus and Inspiration.

Ascend Into Rare Air

By lifting others up all around you
You in return will rise

Like the light above the clouds
Illuminating those who have fallen
From grace so they may stand with pride
There is a connection amongst us all
It flows from one to another as we interact
New beginnings begin to sprout
Growing from enriched waters of positivity

Operate from a state of mind
That going above and beyond is
How everything you do is done
Evolving to a place of always doing more
Regardless of what is only required
Solidifies your standing amongst a select group

Usher in more than you can
Possibly imagine by giving exponentially

Awakenings from those that find themselves
Lost in the abyss of life
Languishing from day to day like driftwood in open waters

Aligns the course of ones purpose
Rousing the soul to a sense of meaning and
Openness to the vast opportunities
Unfolding right in front of you
Nutrients consumed from this source
Directly energize internal power

Your awareness is now heightened to
Ones abilities to impact others opening a
Utopia of purity from breathing rare air

By lifting others up all around you.

Feel You

Something tugs at your soul
Points you in a direction still untold
Intuition shows you the way
Right in front of you the answers lay
Into the depths
Time brings you closer
Undeniably
A pathway step by step this
Lane requires no closure

Can you feel me now
One mind, heart, body, and soul
Never alone
Not even one day
Emptiness has no home to stay
Together for infinity
In this life and the next
On this universe
Nothing can disconnect
Spiritual Connection.

Destination

Every fall provides a way back
Nucleus of a destination the
Journey requires planning and work
One successful step at a time
Your sight should be set on

Take notes along the way
How much progress you make
Embrace the effort

Joy comes not only from the end result
One map and one destination
Use the course set in your mind
Recharge along the way
Never mind small obstacles on the journey
Each one provides a challenge to overcome
Yielding new growth that did not exist before

Enjoy the Journey.

CEO

Challenge the status quo
Hold yourself accountable for everything
Intelligent in common sense
Essential components include leadership
Finding those who posses desired strengths

Executing a plan based on a desired outcome
X factor you bring to the table
Elevate the performance of those around you
Calculated and deliberate in decision making
Unabated in those decisions
Taking advantage of opportunity presented
Invisible to others but not to you
Value the mastermind group
Educated in the power of thought

Opens the mind to a constant state of learning
Forward thinking
Finds solutions, not excuses
I will lead by example
Confidence exudes, assuring in nature
Exemplifying character
Rise to the occasion staying strong in stature

CEO.

Prisoner No More

Use the key within to unlock your mind
So where do we find this key
Everyone is born with it

The origin resides in programming
Held in beliefs from both
External influence and internal thoughts

Kept tucked away in the depths of the mind
Enter by using your power and the key will manifest
You and you alone control your thoughts, your power

With control, this power protects against
Influence of a negative nature and
The way you think about yourself
How you think reflects into reality
It directly portrays who you are
Negative or positive the choice is yours

Thinking is the key and it is the mot powerful
Originator of your life

Unlock all your potential by using it
Neurons of positivity attract others
Linked by the synapses in the subconscious
Oscillating around the imagination
Crafting a vision to pursue
Knowledge and direction flow from this source

Your key is the most important possession
Only to be used by you, and no one else
Under your protection guard it well
Reflect on the cell released from, prison of the

Mind is nothing more than limits and beliefs we
Inherently construct and contain ourselves in
Needlessly restraining all life has and we have to offer
Detained until the day you choose to unlock the door

Use the key within to unlock your mind.

Awakening

Honor it all
On the journey you will fall
Pick yourself up
Encourage just one step

Learning to embrace
On this day, change in you
Valuing the struggle
Evolved to see all the good too

Focused this sight has become
A new perspective
I fear no more
The light is in front of me
Hand of GOD, I have been touched for all to see

Hope, Love , & Faith.

The Secret Key

Whisper in your ear
Every word will define your future

Behold the vision
Each thought will manifest
Content is the key
Openness to your dreams
Making goals to achieve
Empowered in the mind

Wait no more
Hence the hour has arrived
Apprehension will not do
Take what is given for it is a gift

Wake the sleeper
Enter what you want to become

Thinking positive will bring each piece
Hone in on what you desire
I do not fear or worry for the path is set
Needing only belief
Keeping the promise I make to myself

Abundance in life
Bound by only the limits we set
On the launch pad
Undiscovered fulfillment
Ten nine eight seven six five four three two one ignite

We become what we think about.

Faith

Now is not the time
On this day why can I not know
Time must be allowed for the answers to show

How can this be right
A long walk into the night
Venting all my frustrations
Inside a calmness begins to flow
Neediness will need to go
Grace will take its place

Awkward feeling it can be
Lessons have a purpose
Learning them isn't always easy

Tomorrow is an unknown
Honesty will be shown
Even the strongest can fall

A choice all of us have to make
Nothingness or
Stand up one step to take
Walk this path
Everyday anew
Resurrection planted and grew
Smile bright this faith with you

Not having all the answers.

Genesis

The origin of formation

So often we fail before we ever start
Even with good intentions
Leaving the gate we
Fail to prepare for the journey

Course in mind but no navigation
Old habits fight to keep the status quo
Rebellion in the mind
Return to the familiar
Everything will fight you
Conscious planning begins to program
The code will take hold

Begin at the source
Your journey requires

Reinforced positive thinking
Each action needs to be planted
Practice by repetition
Rebalancing will take place
Out with non producing habits
Gravitate to a higher standard
Reduced urges turn to
An increased enjoyment
Mark this step, you are on your way
Maintain a consistency
Increase the throttle the course is set
Now you know how to get to the destination
Gages are synchronized

There comes an anticipation
How is replaced with knowing
Excitement toward results

Stimulates the mind to continue
Origin of formation aligned
Utilizing new information
Reprogrammed for success
Conscious and subconscious in synch
Efficacious now in the results desired

Self correct by reprogramming the source.

Higher Ground

Circumstances can affect us all
Holding us back, keeping us stagnate
Averting hope from our thoughts
Nothing will change, this is my life
Grounded in fear
Excuses are your friend, its not me

You are a victim of circumstance
One very common theme, those who
Use blame to justify their failures
Ready to move out of this existence

Change your circumstances
I choose to control what I can and
Release resentment
Circumstances don't oppress you
U and you alone control your mind
Making your reality what you choose
Start being accountable for it all
There is higher ground and the path
Always starts with thought
Now, you don't like circumstances
Change them!
Easy too say but built on a foundation of truth
Silence any negativity and practice

A positive mental attitude in all situations
Negativity only attracts more of the same
Distance yourself from it

Gravity will pull you toward a better place
Ephemeral when things don't go your way
Transmuting in a constructive manner

The path to higher ground is clear
Open lane appears, signal, and accelerate

Change your circumstances and get to...

Inner Power

There is a feeling inside
Hitting every nerve
Energy building

Finding its way
Lighting a path
Atomic
Multiplying
Enriched by purpose

Wielding it
Inside you, it's source
Truth, lights it's force
Higher and higher
It builds
Needing only belief to fulfill

The flame within.

Vision

My mission is to change lives
Aligning what is with that it can be
Karma fills this place
In walk, roll, or are carried those who are broken
Nourishment is given in the form of hope
Guide me in this quest

Damage can be transformed
Requirements are only belief
Elements come together
And something new is born
Made stronger than the previous version
Specialized in capabilities

Rebuilt for function
Evolved to take the user on
A new journey
Life is given a second chance
In a new form
True beauty has been revealed
Your vision makes dreams into reality

Making dreams reality.

Declaration Of Change

Day begins
I choose to tolerate no more
Seed of change
Content with comfort ends
On a platform of accountability
New habits replace old
They are the definitions of you
Envy has no place
Need to embrace what is uncomfortable
True growth resides here

I choose to reject conformity
Same routine of sterility

The land of familiarity
Holds you in a dead place
Entity of anger for something different

Sound the alarm
Embrace the fear of the unknown
Evidence suggests falsity in being safe
Dare to step forward

Our fears disguised as
False evidence appearing real

Champion strength from above
Home of the stronghold
A battlefield in the mind
New ground to lay the foundation
Gift of a renewed mind
Envelope of positive change addressed to you

Discontent is the seed of change.

Warrior

Under a cloud of hesitation
Number of times you held back
Limits have been set
Each opportunity passes you by
Are you going to stay asleep
Silent when the time confronts
How much longer will you wait

Time runs out, unfulfilled promises
Hopes and dreams forgotten
Enough I think not

Wake, vision is clear
A positive mental attitude arrived
Reach inside and make the choice
Risks must be taken
It all comes down to you
Opportunity will now be pounced on
Reward of self discipline

Widen your range of courage
I can do all things through him
Torch fear and execute
Hardened in my resolve
I will walk into the fire
Needing only faith

Unleash the warrior within.

Go There

The connection between energy and matter
How we communicate to the universe
Our thoughts dock to the mind's launching pad
Upward thrust orbiting ideas
Gaining momentum and mass
Hyper drive activated
The fuel put in must be pure
Space and time find a parallel

Become one
Every cell activated
Can you unlock this power
Outer limits we must go
Multiplying synapses
Elevate to what is possible

Rush of blood stimulates
Entrust in the tools provided
A task each can complete
Learn the process
Intelligence suggests to
Translate problems into advantages
Yielding opportunity

Interpret signs and see
Newly created ideas

They need only planting
Here lies the secret
Each thought will manifest

Make preparations for what is coming
Invest in where you want to go
Now is the time to
Develop both near and far sight
Seize the opportunity in front and ahead

What flows from the source
Once embraced by belief
Reaches the minds workshop
Keep it clean
So it can produce only the finest quality
Hammered with conviction and faith
Originated by imagination
Prevail for that which you have become

Thoughts become reality in the mind's workshop.

I Am

Start each sentence with I am
Introduce words
Linked to positive affirmations
Elevate how you talk to yourself
Not is a word to discard
Thinking in terms of possibilities

Conversations
Orbit around who you want to be
New ways to look at yourself
Ventricles of positivity fill your heart
Events will begin to unfold
Ripples hold signals
Separate out anything not pure
Apply items of strength, wants, desires
Translates into actions
I am going to become
Only finish the statement with positive thoughts
Negative statements work as well, so
Stop putting yourself down

Why continue down a path of disparity
It only keeps you stuck
The way out begins by changing the conversation
Honor yourself

Open dialogues
Universal wisdom injects itself
Reimbursement comes from
Stepping outside your fears
Energizing possibilities
Leaving the past behind
Value only things that bring optimism
Entertain ideas
Structure for your future formed, now build

Silent conversations with ourselves.

Change The View

Masked by a barrier
Are there no other ways
Kept in check by false belief
Eyes are not the only way to see
Shut them and see within

Eyes open and new angles emerge
Vision now shows possibilities
Elongate the horizon
Reflect on past attempts
Your depth of perception increases
There is always a way
Hindsight will prove
It just needed to be found
New pathways open
Grounded in persistence

Pave a way around, over, or through
Obstacles become opportunities
Shifted by point of view
Shadows of success appear
Invisible before
Becoming more and more vivid
Leverage this new knowledge
Eyes fixated on the way to proceed

Makes everything possible.

The Thinking Gap

A choice of three roads
There are degrees of elevation
To each one a different path
It comes down to perspective
Take the low path and problems
Undermine everything in your life
Damage to you because you identify as a victim
Everything is against you

Divert to the middle path
Everyone follows the crowd
Thinking involves what others do
Environment of safety in numbers
Reach but only for what is in grasp
Memories of what could have been
I should have done more
Normal existence suits you just fine
Everyone can't be an eagle
Soaring above

You change lanes
On ramp to the high path
Unlocking your potential
Reward comes from the struggle

Allow positive thoughts to overtake problems
Limits are only how high you decide to fly
Troubles melt away
I do not except the words "I can't"
They only provide motivation
Undiscovered strength to embrace
Discipline and vision guide
Every failure is one step closer to success

Attitude determines your altitude.

There Is Always A Way

You must start with a desire
On a platform of faith
United by suggestion to yourself

Justified by increasing knowledge
Unlocked by the imagination
Supported by a plan
Time to be decisive, make the decision

Habit formed
A mindset of persistence
Value created by like minded partners
Enthusiasm

Take a picture in your mind
Once conceived now believe

Failure one day converted
Into success on another
Negative mental attitude repelled
Divine guidance

Infinite power to achieve
The possibility of the possible

You just have to find it.

The Cleansing

Request Denied
Embrace only that which is positive
Make no room for negativity
Operate from a place of clarity
Value only those things or people
Enriching your life

Wake to a newness
Harness a positive mind
Awareness to what needs to be removed
Take action

Ignore those who only bring down
Shut the door

Thorough with conviction
Once left never to be reengaged
X is the symbol to remove
It is not always easy to let go of
Comfort in that which causes pain

Inner strength you have
Near the core

Yield your power to soar
Out with the time wasters
Up is our direction
Remove, reflect, and rise

Life should not be wasted
It goes by with a blink
Forget what is behind
Embrace what lies ahead

Remove what is toxic in your life.

The Stretch

Rendering a plan
Enter with courage you can
Anticipate failure over and over
Confidence and perseverance needed
Honing in step by step

Figuring out is part of the prep
On and on
Repetition with adjustment, again!

Why is this so hard
How can it be done
Another attempt
There must be a way

I will not give in. I will stay!
Some say why, others don't dare try

One goal at hand
Until it is reached
That is how I will stand

On this journey, fallen so many times
Forging strength during the climb

Going the distance
Reach you are so close
Another try, say yes to persistence
Senses and focus, acute
Power forward success and completion astute

Reach for what is out of grasp.

Purpose Of Failure

There is always a way
One must persist to find it

Reveal, then reflect, then
Entrust in yourself and execute
Vision is the ability to see a path
Even when no one else can
Appreciate failing instead of fearing it
Learn to become excited for you are

One step closer to success
Picture in your mind accomplishing the task
Proclaim, it is just a matter of time
Opportunities are born from every failure
Riches can flow from the discovery
Temporary should always proceed failure
Unlocking the power of persistence
Ninety nine percent won't, so be the one percent that will
Invest in yourself and have conviction
Take the challenging path by choice
You will reveal unknown powers, strength, and capabilities
within

To Reveal Opportunity.

The Switch

Take a deep breath and turn it on

Postponement whispers in the wind
Ripe with excuses
Oculus grows smaller and smaller
Clouded with a comfort zone
Reasons to wait mount
Always another day
Stillness becomes a good friend
Time will always be available
Inconclusive bargains made with the mind
Nebulous initiative hazes focus
Actions and words do not align
Taking you to a destination of nowhere
Inspect the origin
Open and honest discussion with yourself
Now place your finger on the switch

Take a deep breath and turn it
On! This light shines bright

Pour a cup of persistence and drink this
Eternal elixir, consumed regularly
Results in a faith to never quit
Strongest emotions intensifying the
Imagination to form new angles
Shifting the sight forward never back
There is a clear focus
Eyes are fixated I will not cease
Nourishing the soul to get up after each fall
Constructive nature conveyed by dreams
Embodies willfulness to persist until achievement is attained

Procrastination to Persistence.

Battlefield

Voices say stop
I just want to quit
Clouds of doubt fill the mind
Take the easy path
Out of the furnace
Rifts of disbelief
You just can't do it

I push all this away
Stop the quitting thoughts

Wash it away
One more time, keep repeating
Nerves of persistence define your thoughts

I will not stop until I win attitude
Now I begin to understand

There will be setbacks
Heavy knock downs along the way
Each time I get back up

Makes me stronger
I know I get closer each time
New skills and knowledge develop
Distance narrowed, flag of victory ready to be planted

Victory is won in the mind.

Commitment

Nothing starts without it
Or will you let mediocrity grow

Excuses are a chosen nutrient
X them out one by one
Commitment at the core
Uses accountability as the foundation
Show up no more trying just doing
Even when you don't want to

I take ownership of it all
Stop giving reasons

And start producing results
Confidence builds and courage ingrained
Certified by your actions
Entertain the excuses no more
Performance increased
Take responsibility
Avenues of trust open
Begin today
Leave all in the past behind
Embrace the power of you

No excuse is acceptable.

If Not Now Then When

I sit here thinking of all the reasons
Fiction based in normality

New boundaries to explore
Originate the push
The small voice inside says; now

No need to think, just act
On or off
Which way will you turn

Time has brought you to this place
Held down no more
Erupt into action
Need inside grows

Willed into reality
Half determination, half persistence
Equals omnipotence
Now go

If not now then when.

You Are Special

A gift resides inside you
It was placed there just for you
Making you special and unique

Finding your gift is essential
Only you and you alone have it
Render a picture in your mind

What does the silent voice say when you think of it
Have the conversation
Activation requires having applied faith
Traction takes hold with doing not procrastination

Your gift belongs to you and is meant to be shared
Oppress it and it dies with you
Unable to impact and fulfill intention

What will your legacy be
Empty existence or pursuit of life's purpose for you
Rise strong to the occasion and go to work
Explore your imagination using the minds workshop

Magic happens when ambition is added to desire
Apply some willpower and persistence to the
Decision and make it definite
Enthusiasm will multiply the effect

Faith is designed to strengthen the foundation
Overture of belief becomes louder and louder
Right in your sights, now take aim for what you were made for

Aim for what you were made for.

You Will Become

What you think about
How do you think about yourself
Are you always focused on the negative
Then why would you expect to be happy

You see it really is that simple
Our thoughts are our reality
Until they change life will not

There is an abundant life waiting for you
Here are the steps to take
Incorporate only positives, they exist all around you
No more "nothing works out for me"
Kick it out of your mind every time it knocks

Always and I mean always focus on what you want
Be optimistic in the face of adversity
Out of it lies opportunity and purpose
Unlock the door marked desires, seeds of
Thought will plant and grow into a harvest for life to flow

What you think about.

Go With The Flow

Release rigidity
Elevate yourself to a clear lane
Lose mental baggage
Ease your mind
And allow clarity
Synchronicity glides with awareness

Richly awarded
Intuition operating
Grounded in applied faith
Induced to go the extra mile
Directional signs appear in advance
Inspiring all that is needed
To appear at the right time
Yielding that which you desire

Release Rigidity.

It's Not Easy But ... The Answer Is Simple

Change the conversations you
Have with yourself
Answers you already have
Need to be affirmed
Go toward positive changes you want
Empty out negative ways

You don't need to put yourself down
Orbit around who you want to be
Unleash yourself
Remember you are special

There is peace inside you
How many times have
I'm not good enough thoughts led to
Needless acts of hesitation
Kick them out!
Increase this awareness
New beginnings start with "I am"
Grateful for who I am and new ways I'm going to think

Change your thinking.

Action

Imagination is where it starts
Dreams of an ideal take shape
Events in the mind paint a picture
Aspiring to create a reality
So much potential

Attentive and focused in the moment
Ripe for action to be taken
Evaporate in a split second

Withheld by procrastination
Or just a laziness to move
Regretted years later
Time found another to act
Hidden in plain sight
Lenses with the proper prescription
Evaluate the steps to be taken
See with focus by adjusting the
Shutter to let ideas flow

Unite the idea with action
Now a plan can be formed
Learn to prepare for each step
Events will unfold when ready to receive
Something you never had will require
Something you've never done

Action is a choice
Choose to take it
The alternative is where ideas
Enter a mental tomb, only to be
Discovered by another

Use what has been given
Propel yourself forward
Open the mind and let it work
Now is the time as the idea becomes reality

Ideas are worthless unless acted upon.

Extreme Focus

Enter a state of trance
No external influences
Tune in to the task at hand
Extreme focus
Requires all distractions dissipated

Activation and acceleration

Saturated in fixation
The entryway to flow opened
Abilities enhanced
Time slows
Every fiber aligned in purpose

One voice speaks
Funneling thoughts

Turning the task into realization
Resources are infinite
Alive like never before
Nerve endings firing in synchronization
Capturing the target
Elation

Enter a state of trance.

Desire

Tugs at your soul
Honesty at the core
A little voice inside won't go away
This belongs to you and no one else

Waiting to be acted upon
How do I start
I don't know the way
Catapult your mind into action
Hone in on clues

You don't have to have all the answers
Once belief takes hold
Undone only by an unwillingness to act

Activate the doorway
Remember only you can walk through
Empty the well and refill

Source a new energy
Every step of faith strengthens
Apply principles of truth
Reach for that which is out of grasp
Choose wisely who you dialog with
Honor those who embrace
I choose my own path
Nothing is more powerful or
Greater than a changed mind

It guides us with purpose
Solidified with a goal

Are you committed
Learn from those before
Seek knowledge
Our capacity is limitless

Seek for it is seeking you
Eye on the prize
A flow brings that which is needed
Rich in energy
Capable of all given to it
Hidden in plain sight
Its really up to you
Nothing more than a choice
Grounded or rise

Focus and pursue
Open and aware of all that surrounds you
Render it in your mind

You can picture it already done
One dream, one goal, one purpose
Unified and delivered

That which you are searching is also searching for you.

62

Something More

False sense of accomplishment
Allow yourself to give up
It can't be done
Languish in excuses
Unable to see past a failed result
Rearview mirror always in front
Employed by doubt

View begins to change
Enroll in a new way
Resist the naysayer
Stare at the reflection
Undo the failed mindset
So much potential to unleash

Success is a process
Unwavering belief in you
Can be done attitude
Coffin is a place for excuses
Each failure teaches something
Step closer to achievement
Something more is all that is needed

Failure versus success.

Driven

Dedicated on a level few understand
Invested above and beyond
Force equals mass multiplied by acceleration
Finding a higher level to operate
Energy comes from a source above
Respect is earned by actions
Elevated with the work I put in
Need that only I can fill
Comfort has no place with me
Each action has a purpose

Making the whole stronger
Are you willing to go there
Kept in a place for only the worthy
Evoking this power to excel
Right and left hemispheres fixated on the target

Difference maker.

Abundant Life

Each day starts with gratitude
Value all that has been given
Even pain serves a greater purpose
Richness comes from the journey
Yearn for a greatness inside
Travel beyond the familiar
Have a positive attitude even
In times of adversity and struggle
Neglected self care works against
Goals proceeded by action

New ways of thinking
Everyday is a blessing
Enriched by those around you
Discovering capabilities
Events of my life happen to teach
Dictated by the steps I take

I represent the beauty inside us all
Shall I walk this path to show

An abundant life led by grace
Learn to recognize the good in each
Rise today with anticipation
Eyes choose to see what they want
Afraid of only stagnation
Discard the fears and be brave
You are the director and writer

In these pages the story of you
New chapters to write
Silhouette of colors
Illuminate from this book
Distance from happiness
Eludes only from thought

Like Yohana Estrade
Everything needed is already inside.

Manifestation

The power of thought resides
Holding you back is only disbelief
Every cell works together

Signals transmit that which we desire
Unlocked by inner thoughts
Bound together
Conduits bring back what is sent out
On this platform we build
Negativity need not apply
Signs will appear to follow
Circuits direct
Intuition let be your guide
One purpose transmit
Unlock this power
Something so strong it cannot be denied

Manifest what you desire
In your mind picture it
Nerve endings will catch fire
Dictate, develop, define, drive

The Subconscious Mind.

Inflection Point

Rendering of your life at this point
Entering a new phase
Considering all that has been learned
One moment
Grasp the opportunity
Now is the time
Intuition is your guide
Zone of change
Engulfed with certainty

The direction becomes clear
How far have you come
Elevated in thought

Take this turn
Undiscovered
Right in front of you
Nothing to fear but fear itself

Recognize the turn …

Stepping Stones

Seeds of advantage come from adversity
Temporary is a key word to use
After defeat and treat it as so
It is not easy but
Repeated over and over by trying again
Wins the mind over
Attempt after attempt
Yields clues and areas to make adjustments

Turns trying into doing
Often we give up too soon

Success only needs one good reason
Useless are hundreds of can't be done ones
Can is a word of belief
Confidence grows out of the seed of advantage
Embracing failure is something to learn from
Steps are crafted each time creating your
Stairway to success.

Drop The Hammer

Fire up your internal forge
Once warmed up
Raise the intensity
Grab your hammer and form
Each point of contact transforms

There is a desire inside you
One more repeated, forms a habit to

Break through limits
Untapped until now
I am powerful and I will go there
Lean into it and apply leverage
Drive forward and conquer

Forge to build.

Mindset

Yield a crop planted with mental seeds
On a field of desire
Up to you what grows
Ripened with truth

Make it your foundation and
Every seed will grow for good
Newness in life comes from the mind
The relationship between subconscious thought
And conscious reality
Learn to plant only the positive

Water it from the fountain of the universe
Open the valve
Remember what was planted either good or bad will prosper
Keep weeds of doubt from taking hold
Spray them with belief
Harmonize with the nature of your desire
Once grown a crop fertilized from
Planted thoughts of the mind

Your mental workshop.

The Passenger

To follow blindly
A path not set by you
Kept in a controlled state
Emptiness but comfort

Can I make the leap
Or stay confined with the herd
Now or never
Take the reigns
Regrets left behind
Our lives are a journey
Lead with faith built by confidence

Our time here is short
Flashes by with a blink

You have strength undiscovered
Only found with courage
Unfold the map
Ready to chart the course

Leave all that is negative on the dock
I believe in me
Follow no more
Every step from here is mine to take

Take control of your life.

The Essence Of Change

Beginnings new are locked
Remembering old ways of thinking
Embrace only old ways of doing
A dismantling must occur
Keeping a hold will not do
Deep in this mirror a reflection of you
One on one a conversation
With me
Now a decision must be made
Stay in this place, same results played

Crying out loud, I've had enough
Rip this wall down
Every brick must fall
A collapse has occurred
The hour at hand
Enlightened

Begin to stand
Rejoice in this moment
Evolving into the new
A mindset has broken
Keeping you in that old place
Time to leave to a life fulfilling space
Hone in on a new way
Right here starting today
One mind cleared of the old
Until now you were not bold
Growing isn't always easy
Heightened you have become
Successful transformation equals the sum

Remember: Breakdowns Create Breakthroughs.

Attainment Principle

Begin by picturing it in your mind
Escalate by concentration
Link the two together
Imagine it already in your possession
Enlist your mind to go to work
Voice from within will guide
Each step toward attainment

Abundant mindset is a magnetic state of attraction
Not a state of fear based on scarcity
Drone out these thoughts by expecting

All that is good to start coming your way
Capitalize on what is right in front of you
Hidden in plain sight
I have come to learn the
Essential ingredient that separate a
Vast and impactful life from one of
Emptiness is the power to control thought

Believe and Achieve.

The Compounding Effect

Excellence through repetition
X 1000 may be the number needed to
Calculate success in this
Equation of the mind
Lines of achievement need to be established
Let us begin with a self assessment
Evaluate both strengths and weaknesses
Needed skills to acquire will assist in
Crafting a plan to follow
Each action must have a purpose

There will be clues along the way
Highlight areas that work and
Remove areas that don't
Our plan is becoming more refined
Useless items discarded, we are now
Grounded in a mastery process
Hold on we are about to accelerate by

Raising the bar, refining, and repeating
Every dividend received is reinvested
Producing the compounding effect
Interest build upon itself
The formula is built by design
Investing in yourself produces the
Transformation and result
Internal strength has increased exponentially
One step built upon another as a repeating cycle
Now complete and ingrained in you a process of excellence to
template

Excellence Through Repetition.

Whispers From Above

Ever get that tingling sensation
Volts of sensation stimulate in effervesce
A voice whispers to either confirm or warn
Navigators in time of need
Grappling with a decision
Evaluators with a sixth sense
Listen from within
Instruments to hear reside there
Can you hear me now
Always know I am here with you
Let the light shine down upon you

Guidance is meant to both validate and resurrect faith
Understand the nature of my purpose
I am here to show a way when blinded
Demonstrated with love for goodness
Never fear an end for a new start always follows
Can you feel me now as you are fully
Embraced with my grace

Evangelical Guidance.

All Aboard

Limits are set in the mind by allowing
External views from others to construct
A stop sign planted as false evidence appearing real
Disregard comments that discourage
So few can walk in faith and cast away fear

Truth shows they can't exist together
Only fear can smother out a burning desire

Shutting down your initiative to act
Used as an excuse to bathe in mediocrity
Cast all fears away by first self examining
Causes from the root source
External beliefs that limit the ability to
See that all things are possible
Once saturated in the mind's workshop of belief

And conceived from the imagination
Nurture a way of seeing beyond
Dismantle a limit by breaking down the parts

Analyze areas of weakness within to strengthen
Begin building those areas up
Understanding and now believing it is possible
Now stare the limit down and it will fear you
Deer in headlights the limit has no idea
As you are about to break right through like a train
Catapulting it into nonexistence
Evolution of this process completed and emerged a stronger
version of you
Now follow these tracks and accelerate the limits will get out of
the way

Leads to Success and Abundance.

Persistence Test

Pay a price you must
An abundance of prosperity awaits
So why do so few make it
Simply put most can't take it

There is an ingredient that
Has the ability to break down barriers
Eventually the gatekeepers give up

Proclaiming they have had enough
Epic ability to keep going no matter what
Raises the eyebrows of the universe
Surrendering the prize wrapped with persistence
Into the abyss
Silence and darkness surround
Temptations allure to quit entices
Escape this place
Ninety nine out of one hundred will
Cave in and end the pursuit
Everyone else is not you though

Take the hit and keep going
Emboldened after each temporary defeat
Shining light inside you will not be denied
Those who know their destination and won't stop pass the test

Pass the Persistence Test.

You Never Know How Much Time You Have

You never know how much time you have
Our clocks are all set the same to start
Unseen is the amount we have to use

Never until it is too late, time runs out
Each of us must decide what we do with it
Venture out and experience it all
Every up and every down
Receive an abundance by giving in abundance

Know and use the moral compass as a guide
Never take the simple things for granted
Only to regret it later
Withholding only takes from you

How much can you take with you
Only dust so why hold back
What aspirations do you have and how

Much are you willing to give to get
Usher in a fulfilling life
Create a purpose and pursue
Hold dear and cherish all the moments

Time is not an unlimited resource
It can not be given back
Make an effort to see the good all around
Each life you impact will impact another

You are the star in your own movie called life
Operate as writer and director
Unhappy, then rewrite the scene

Have courage to embrace it all
Always lift others up as it will lift you as well
Value the feeling of loving unconditionally
Enjoy, give, persist, discover, and plant positive seeds to harvest
an abundant life

You never know how much time you have.

Dinner With Destiny

Make a reservation with your destiny
Entry requires a gift from within
No need to worry you were born with it
Unique and beautifully wrapped by you

Invite some friends to this dinner as well
Their names are persistence, imagination, and initiative
Each has a part to play and will
Motivate you with willpower and positivity
So make sure to invite them as well

Inspired the chef has added something special
New menu items are rare but this is no ordinary dinner
Conceived with knowledge and passed down from wisdom
Lets leave it for latter in tonight's courses
Uninvited are doubts and fears, they are not welcome
Dinning with your destiny is a privilege
Each course plays a pivotal part, so lets eat

Desire
Establishes a want that must be filled
Spend a little more on desire, let it sink in
Inner conversations will solidify and
Reinforce this attainment principle
Establishing a nice epicure with destiny lets try some

Faith
Appetite for this menu item tonight
Increases with every bite, indulge
The more you have will
Honor a commitment to your destiny

A definite chief aim, our chef's mystery dish
Now has arrived but not last, for once consumed and fully
Digested it must be followed by

Belief
Entirety throughout your soul as this course completes
Leave doubt and fear outside
Inevitably they will try and crash this dinner
Effectively denied entry by the
Four courses of desire, faith, definite chief aim, and last but not
least belief

Menu items include Desire, Faith, and Belief.

From My Heart

From the Heart
My affirmation to you

Feeling and emotion triangulate
Engulfing every nerve
Each word has significant meaning
Let it flow from me to you
I share it expecting nothing in return
Needing only to lift others instilling hope
Gratified by a smile and new light

As the gift has been welcomed and embraced
Noble and pure intentions
Disseminate from every pour to

Enlist a higher calling for you
Movement and actions align
Offering comfort and a path forward
Take this offering let it fill your heart
In the process you will fill mine
Overflowing, pass it on to another
Never-ending connectivity, healing heart, mind, and soul.